Accidentals on Purpose

A Musician's Dictionary

INDENT
PUBLISHING

Accidentals on Purpose

A Musician's Dictionary

By David W. Barber

Cartoons
Dave Donald

☐INDENT
PUBLISHING

ACCIDENTALS ON PURPOSE:
A Musician's Dictionary

First published in Canada in 2011

INDENT PUBLISHING
121 Shanly St.
Toronto, ON, Canada M6H 1S8
indentpublishing.com
contact@indentpublishing.com

This edition first printing, September 2011

Canadian Cataloguing in Publication Data

Barber, David W. (David William)
Accidentals on Purpose

ISBN 978-0-9809167-2-0

1. Music - History - Anecdotes, facetiae, satire, etc.
2. Composers - Anecdotes, facetiae, satire, etc.
1. Donald, David C. 11. Title

ML65.B37 1986 780'.9 C86-093755-0

Typeset in Century Expanded

AUTHOR'S NOTE
AND ACKNOWLEDGEMENTS

As work progressed on this book and before I had decided upon its title, I grew tired of having constantly to refer to it as "my book" or "the book I'm working on." And so it came to be known simply as Sam — which doesn't stand for anything. It was just that I already had a book named Fred in the works, and Sam was more polite than "hey you." And so it is as Sam that I still know it. It still usually answers to that name.

Observant readers will notice this new edition contains definitions and illustrations culled from my earlier opera dictionary, *Tenors, Tantrums and Trills.* Congratulations — move to the head of the class.

There are many people who — by way of advice, encouragement or otherwise — were helpful at various stages in the production of this book. To them I offer my warmest acknowledgements and thanks. Chief among these are the members of my family and my friends for their support and encouragement. And thanks to Jacques Lauzon of Indent Publishing and to Dave Donald for their help in this revised and expanded edition.

DWB
Westport and Toronto, 1997, 2011

PREFACE

Those wedded to music belong to the realm of the constant-ephemeral — a visionary realm requiring oft-time the painful renunciation of reality — remember those glorious images of spirit rendered flesh — of divinity — of beauty of princes and princesses condemned to a yearning for even the shortest-lived mortal incarnation — and oft-times lending that alternative dimension, introspective or objective, as the case may be, to one's own life.

A musician's humor is the inevitable distillation of a capacity to listen to himself, honestly to take blame for his own mistakes and shortcomings, a freedom from prejudice and an ability to see himself in as unreal and ludicrous a light as others might see him, this extra-terrestrial being — messenger, clown, seer, priest or demon — exposing and liberating us to ourselves in the deepest sense possible and without the accusatory embarrassment of words. For humor is the gift of the gods — born of deep humanity, of suffering and compassion, as of that divine and somewhat remote disattachment it promotes the same creative originality of observation which reveals the mysteries of Nature to the born scientist as the mysteries of human nature to the born artist.

Musicians are, generally, irrepressible in their exuberance, passion and curiosity. Usually, if they are real musicians, they are, as such, essential and irresistible to their mortal fellow-women and fellow-men. They form a curious breed blessed with the eye and ear of the beholder, thus able to make fun of themselves and perhaps, more through humor than philosophy, cheat, if only fleetingly, the very powers of darkness and tragedy which stalk the path of life.

This amusing and witty book has only one omission, i.e. the pianist, who, as a genuinely profound musician taking my teasing in good grace, must be a magician. Having a brilliant pianist as my son (Jeremy by name) my imagination has been exhaustively exercised in commenting — of course disparagingly (for that is the very essence of humor) — on this out-of-tune piece of furniture, which can serve in so many other capacities than music — for instance a bar or nice flat surface to stretch out on, as the case may be. Shark-like it displays a menacing lower denture of black and white teeth; a more rational disposition of this lower denture in the proper half-circle has been tried but abandoned, no doubt owing to the increased difficulty of turning pages — also called keyboard, to which the pianist, countering with an upper denture of ill-fitting and bleeding fingers, hammers and grinds out (with the help of additional hammers hidden in the bowels of the beast) a percussive noise of simultaneous notes, called harmony — obviously so dubbed because these notes are in fact short-lived, falsely pitched, aggressive. Therefore the great pianist is, as I tell my son Jeremy, a good magician, for by sheer will and imagination he conveys the ecstasy of music through means which are therefore a compromise. The keyboard has never developed into a proper typewriter, for the alphabet is unmarked and in no case extends beyond the letter G, and it is further devoid of numerals. For these reasons pianists do not make successful secretaries. I am in no doubt that the publisher is reserving an entire book on this vast subject.

And now, having attempted to throw a spadeful of grit into this delightful book, may I offer my best wishes to the reader, who will share and perchance enjoy a sample of musician's humor — from one of this laugh-able stock.

Yehudi Menuhin

DEDICATION

For Brian Law, who first taught me
that music can laugh, with all due respect.

Le monde est plein de fous,
et qui n'en veut pas voir,
doit se tenir tout seul,
et casser son miroir.

Thomas Love Peacock
(*Crotchet Castle*, 1831)

And for Judy/Astrid, for everything she has done over
the years to help, support and encourage me.

Per ardua ad Astrid

A

Abandon 1. A term to describe singing or playing of a wild, uncontrolled nature, as often found in opera, modern music and bad student recitals.
2. The best thing to do to musicians performing in this manner.

Abduction 1. A common operatic plot device (Mozart's *Abduction from the Seraglio*, Britten's *The Rape of Lucretia* and others) in which a singer is forcibly removed from the scene.
2. An event some opera- or concertgoers think should happen more often — especially if kidnapping is the only way to get some really lousy performer off the stage.

Accent 1. A musical or rhythmic stress, as on the first beat of a bar.
2. What many musicians speak with.

Accidentals Wrong notes. Notes of pitches other than those indicated by the key signature. In other words, the polite term for mistakes, made by either the performer or composer. Confusingly, some accidentals are done on purpose.

Achilles An ancient Greek hero, betrothed to Iphigenia (in Gluck's *Iphigenia in Aulis* and others). Unfaithful at first, he later rescues the heroine — proving he's not such a heel after all.

Acoustics The science of sound, and the study

of how music misbehaves in various physical environments. Most useful as a scapegoat to explain why the performer(s) sound bad — "How can anyone perform in a space like this?" and so on.

Action In a piano, the term used to describe the behavior of the mechanism that produces the sound. The action may be considered "light," "heavy," "stiff" and so on. Also, the term a pianist might use to describe activities that are more recreational in nature. This sort of action might be considered "slow," "hot," "lucky" and so on.

Addio Italian for "goodbye." A term often found in operatic arias (*Addio alla madre*, from Mascagni's *Cavalleria Rusticana*; *Addio, fiorito asil*, Pinkerton's farewell from Puccini's *Madama Butterfly*; *O terra, addio*, from Verdi's *Aida* and so on). Sung at great length by performers before they actually leave. Sometimes this takes forever.

Ad libitum From the Latin "at liberty," a style of music improvised or delivered freely, at the discretion of the performer. Often displayed by soloists in cadenzas and the repeat sections of *da capo* arias. Not to be confused with "add Librium," a medicinal prescription often advisable (for conductors and other listeners) at such times.

Affections 1. The feelings or emotions of music. In the late Baroque, these were codified into a doctrine of compositional technique.
2. Emotions often on display in musical performances, between soloists and instrumentalists, among chorus members and so on. Often likely to prove awkward and inconvenient when they sour.

Aida A big, splashy opera by Giuseppi Verdi — you know, the one with the elephants. Commissioned in 1870 by the Khedive of Egypt to open the Suez Canal,

Aida

Aida was not actually performed until a year after the party was over, thereby helping to maintain the long tradition of musicians never being ready on time.

Air 1. A simple tune, often for a singer.
2. What the singer must have before performing such a tune.

3. In the plural (airs), what the singer puts on after performing such a tune particularly well.

Alberich A misshapen, ugly Nibelung dwarf, one of the central characters in Wagner's *Ring* cycle. (In three of the four operas, anyway. He gets to sit out *Die Walküre*.) He later turns into a toad, which generally improves his looks.

Aleatoric music Any form of music composition (but especially in modern music) that relies on elements of chance for its production — such as provided by the tossing of coins, throwing of dice or disbursement of artistic grants.

Altered chord Any chord (also called a chromatic chord) that contains notes other than those found in the diatonic scale of the appropriate key. In other words, a chord with wrong notes in it. Occurs frequently in jazz music, modern music and any music involving amateurs and/or small children.

Alto A medium vocal range, lying between tenor and soprano. (A dangerous place to be.) Usually sung by women (see Contralto) but sometimes by men (see Counter-tenor).

Amen The final word of hymns, psalms and many other religious pieces of music (originally from the Hebrew term meaning "so be it" or "you don't say?"). A traditional expression of praise and thanksgiving, the musical and liturgical equivalent of saying "Enough already. Let's just go home." Much more often to be heard from audience members grateful at finally being allowed to leave.

Anacrusis An unstressed note at the beginning of a musical phrase. Also called a pickup note. Not to be confused with anacrisis, a term that might apply when a performer misses the entry on such a pickup note.

Analysis 1. A fruitless attempt at musical dissection, similar to autopsy — the result in both cases being a lifeless, dismembered corpse. The practice of music analysis is based on George Bernard Shaw's precept that "He who can, does. He who cannot, teaches." 2. What's required by many musicians, especially those who've studied music analysis.

Ancora An Italian term meaning "still" (*ancora forte*, still loud) or sometimes "again" (similar to encore). Not to be confused with angora, a type of wool much favored by some musicians for their sweaters.

Answer The second melody in a fugue — which seems to imply the first ought to be considered a question.

Anticipation The sounding of one note before that of the others. A highbrow and more polite term for wrong entry or coming in too soon. Also, the feeling a musician gets while waiting for money to arrive in the mail. (Not to be confused with disappointment, the feeling the musician gets when the amount is smaller than anticipated.)

Applause Noise made by the audience (often at the wrong time, such as in the middle of a symphony, between movements). Intended to signify congratulations, it's used almost as often to destroy the mood of a quiet piece of music, and to express a desire to end the performance and go home.

Aria 1. What you get when you multiply a musician's length by width. 2. A fancy, highfalutin Italian word that just means "song," used by opera and other classical music types to try to impress other opera and other classical music types (such music being essentially nothing more than a glorified form of oneupmanship anyway).

Artistic grants Huge sums of money given at the drop of a hat for useless musical endeavors. They are always given to *other* musicians.

Arts council The living embodiment of Murphy's Law ("If something can go wrong, it will") and the paramount example of Man's inhumanity to Man.

ASCAP An association (the American Society of Composers, Authors and Publishers) founded in 1914 to represent the rights of its members. Not to be confused with dunce cap, an article many of them probably ought to be wearing.

Audience participation

Atonality A pathological disease that affects many composers of modern music. Its most noticeable symptom is the inability to make decisions — such as what key we should be in. It's the advanced and sometimes fatal stage of polytonality.

Audience A group consisting of individuals who, when afflicted by a cold, don't go to a doctor. They go instead to the concert hall, where they hack and wheeze to their heart's content. Audiences can be divided into two categories: Those who sleep with their mouths open and those who sleep with their mouths closed.

B

Bach, J.S. A German Baroque musician, considered by many to be the greatest composer who ever lived. He wrote no operas at all, which must have something to do with it.

Bagpipes A Scottish instrument (of torture, war, mass destruction) whose sound resembles that of a cat being run over by a car. This poses an interesting chronological paradox, since the bagpipes were invented long before the arrival of the automobile. Historians with nothing better to do might consider this a useful thesis topic.

Balance 1. A state of musical equilibrium difficult but essential to attain among groups of singers and instrumentalists
2. A state of mental equilibrium even more difficult but essential to attain among groups of singers and instrumentalists.

Ballad opera A type of light opera especially popular in 18th-century England (such as *The Beggar's Opera*) in which all the tunes are stolen from somewhere else. More accurately, one in which the tunes are openly *admitted* to have been stolen from somewhere else.

Ballet A formal style of dance sometimes found in opera to give the singers a break from the music and the audience a break from the singers.

Band Any group of instrumentalists, but especially those playing rock music or military tunes. Not to be confused with banned — which is what we might wish such groups would be.

Bar 1. The basic measurement of music, dividing it into sections of an approximately equal number of beats, based on the reasonable assumption that musicians can't count higher than four.

2. A place of camaraderie and alcoholic consumption often frequented by musicians (and singers) before, during and after a performance.

Baritone The male voice that lies between the bass and tenor (not unlike a shortstop in baseball), combining the negative qualities of both. Baritones have a ten-

A Baroque composer

dency to sing a different piece of music from everyone else, and to sound like a trombone filled with cold coffee. The term is possibly derived from the Latin *boro*, which means "dunce." Most of those who think they are tenors are actually baritones, just as most baritones are really basses. Found in opera, oratorio and elsewhere, singing such supporting roles as Old Man, Second Fool, Hero's Friend and so on. Rarely gets the girl.

Baroque 1. A period of music so called because the study of it leads to impoverishment.
2. A slang term of encouragement used by musicians. Best exemplified by the phrase "Go for Baroque."

Bartered Bride, The An opera in three acts by Czech composer Bedrich Smetana. An earlier version, now lost, *The Battered Bride*, tells the tragic story of a clumsy waitress in a Prague pancake house.

Bass The lowest vocal line, sung by men, usually old and doddering, often also blind and deaf. Basses have a tendency to sing flat, or not at all, and to sound like a pregnant foghorn. Derived from the Latin *bassus*, which means "base" (but whether in the sense of "pedestal" or "debauched" isn't entirely clear). In opera, the bass is rarely the hero, but often sings an important role as villain or chief buffoon — either of which is ideally suited.

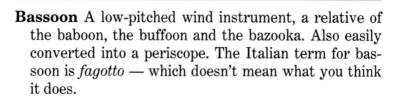

Bassoon A low-pitched wind instrument, a relative of the baboon, the buffoon and the bazooka. Also easily converted into a periscope. The Italian term for bassoon is *fagotto* — which doesn't mean what you think it does.

Baton The thin white stick used by conductors to establish the beat. Thought to have been derived from some sort of ancient fertility symbol, it's now used chiefly out of longstanding tradition. In fact, it's almost utterly useless, since nobody can actually see it. It is useful, however, for threatening recalcitrant musicians or singers, and ought to be sharpened regularly. Derived from the Latin *bastum*, from which we also get the word "bastard."

Bayreuth (see Hell).

Beat 1. The basic unit of measurement in music. It varies from piece to piece, from performance to performance and from person to person. Using a complicated algebraic formula — based on sum totals, averages and phases of the moon — the beat is established by the conductor, and then promptly ignored by all.
2. What a performer is after a performance.

Bebung A rapid trill or vibrato (from the German for "trembling") on a string instrument or sometimes a clavichord. Beethoven and Chopin called for *bebung* in some of their piano pieces, but they were dreaming. You can't do it on a piano. Not to be confused with bebop, a style of music in which any trembling more likely comes from alcohol or drug abuse.

Beggar's Opera, The A famous ballad opera with dialogue and verses by John Gay and music "arranged" (that is, stolen) by John Christopher Pepusch. First performed, to enormous success, in London in 1728. Gay and Pepusch had less success with their

HAVə tENor, SOPrANO, contrALto, and BASS to Fəəd!

little-known followup sequel, *The Beggars-Can't-Be-Choosers Opera.*

Bel Canto A style of singing idealized in opera and fancy concerts (from the Italian for "beautiful song") but rarely found there. Not to be confused with *Can belto,* an inferior style much more often encountered.

Belly 1. In instruments such as the cello, the frontal curved surface over which the strings are stretched. 2. In singers, the frontal curved surface over which the shirt buttons are stretched.

Bent A term used to describe the shape of most valved brass instruments — trumpets, tuba, trombone and so on. By extension, then, the term is often applied to anyone who plays such an instrument (see Heel, Nut).

Bizet, Georges A 19th-century French composer best known for the opera *Carmen.* Not to be confused with bidet, which is something else again.

Bladder-pipe 1. An ancient instrument similar in sound and appearance to a bagpipe. Rarely found in modern music. 2. A surgical device that would prove useful to those having to sit through unbearably long performances, especially of modern music.

Bore 1. In brass and woodwind instruments, the term used to describe the passageway through which air travels — generally either cylindrical or conical. 2. In musicians, the term used to describe many of them.

Bow 1. (Rhymes with go.) A slightly bent device for scraping sound out of a violin. 2. (Rhymes with cow.) A slightly bent gesture for scraping sympathy out of an audience.

Brain A large human organ that controls thought and reason. Distinguishes Man from lower animals and musicians from the rest of mankind. In accordance with the principles of the theory of natural selection and evolution, the cranial space normally reserved for the brain is, in musicians, given over to lung capacity (so that they have, quite literally, blown their brains out). In singers, the absence of brain matter leaves extra room for resonance. Science has been unable to discover whether conductors have been provided with any sort of replacement for the missing brain — but that's highly unlikely.

Brass 1. A family of orchestral instruments that includes trumpets, trombones, French horns and antique bedsteads. The development of brass instruments can be traced back to early 12th-century cisterns. Sound is produced by means of blowing or buzzing (the so-called "raspberry" or "Bronx cheer") into one end of a long, curved tube, in the hopes that the sound that comes out the other end will be less rude. In between may be any number of valves, crooks, spigots, etc. In essence, brass instruments are nothing more than elaborate spittoons.
2. Richard Strauss had this piece of advice for would-be conductors: "Never, under any circumstances, *never* look at the brass."

Break A term with a variety of musical meanings:
1. The point in a singer's voice between the low and high registers.
2. A similar point in the register of many instruments, especially woodwinds.
3. In jazz music, the name for a middle section where a player might perform a solo.
4. In all forms of music, the name for the short rest during rehearsal, strictly enforced by union regulations.
5. In all forms of music, what you might wish to do to an instrument being performed badly — or to the person

doing the performing.

Bridge 1. The middle section of a piece of music that links the opening statement to its return in the recapitulation. 2. A small, arched piece of wood in the violin and other instruments that supports the strings. 3. A game of cards usually more enjoyable than the music of the violin or other string instruments — and an especially useful pastime if the middle section of a piece of music goes on far too long.

Bright With many singers, especially sopranos or tenors, a term that may be used to describe their sound quality — though rarely their intelligence.

Brünnhilde In Norse mythology and Wagner's *Ring* cycle, the daughter of Wotan and the leader of the Valkyries. A big, strapping blonde in a horned helmet and breastplate, she likes to come across as a tough, pushy broad. But at heart she's just Daddy's Little Girl.

Buffa The Italian adjective meaning "comic." (See Opera buffa.) As a noun, more often in the masculine form, *Buffo*, it refers to the singer playing a comic role in an opera. Not to be confused with boffo, which is what producers want the box-office results to be.

Byrd An important figure in the history of early English music (William Byrd, 1543-1623). So important, in fact, that many people consider early English music to be strictly "for the byrds."

C

Cadence A device for stopping a piece of music, the musical equivalent of a brick wall. Some cadences are less complete than others, and may be called "deceptive" or "unfair" cadences. The most common form of cadence is the one called "V-I." In order to understand this, it's necessary to understand the terms "V" and "I." Sorry, can't help you.

Cadenza An elaborate section at the end of a concerto or aria, often improvised, in which performers get to show off the scales and exercises they've been practising for all these years. Not to be confused with credenza, a piece of furniture often far more beautiful and useful than anything they might possibly produce.

Cage, John A 20th-century American composer known for highly experimental and unusual style. His famous piece *4'33"* consists entirely of silence — which would seem to make it ideally suited for adaptation as an opera (and at about the right length, too).

Calore An Italian musical term meaning "heat" or "passion." Not to be confused with calories, the energy value of food consumed in great quantities by some musicians.

Carmen A popular opera by French composer Georges Bizet and the only one ever written about cigarette smugglers. Obviously composed before the introduction of federal laws and tough industry guidelines regulating undue glamorization of smoking and tobacco products.

Carmen

Carol The name of a woman I once knew who — oh, never mind.

Caruso, Enrico A famous Italian operatic tenor of the late 19th and early 20th centuries who earned a worldwide reputation in heroic roles. No relation to Robinson Crusoe, the guy who washed up on a desert island, though some might have wanted them to trade places.

Castrato A male singer surgically altered to retain the upper vocal range. The popularity of the *castrati* reached great heights (you should pardon the pun) in the 18th-century operas of Handel, Porpora and others, even Mozart and Rossini. Now considered illegal in most civilized countries — and even America. The *castrato* often sang heroic roles and got the girl — but had no idea what to do with her.

Cello A member of the string family, larger than both the violin and the viola. The cello is the instrument said to resemble the human voice most closely. However, it has been unable so far to grasp even the most basic principles of grammar and syntax. This is unfortunate, since its incapacity for witty conversation precludes what might otherwise have been an enjoyable lifestyle spent at dinner parties and on the talkshow circuit.

Chest A part of the human anatomy favored by some singers to produce a full, dark tone — and by others just to get attention.

Choir A musical organization thought to have been invented by G.F. Handel to ensure the perpetuation of performances of *Messiah*.

Church 1. That institution largely responsible for the existence of choirs, choirmasters, organs and organists. It's also to blame for sermons, offertories and other forms of punishment.
2. The large, damp, drafty edifice that houses any or all of the above.

Coda A short section of music tacked on to the end of a

piece. The musical equivalent of "P.S."

Comic opera The general term for operas with funny situations and happy endings. Despite the name, they are not actually based on material from comic books, although in most cases the characters are no less cartoonish.

Coloratura soprano A soprano with hiccups.

Comodo A tempo indication (from the Italian meaning "leisurely" or "without strain"). Not to be confused with commode, a small chair containing a chamber-pot — the use of which may also be leisurely (and, one hopes, without strain).

Compass 1. Another term for range — that is, all the notes, from the lowest to highest, than an instrument is capable of playing, or a singer singing. Doesn't include screeches or squawks.
2. A device used by campers, to avoid becoming lost.

Unfortunately not applicable to musicians, except while on tour.

Composer The individual, preferably now dead (the longer the better, up to a point), who was responsible for writing the music. All of the composer's wishes regarding notes, tempo, expression and so are carefully taken down in the score, and then ignored.

Concert hall A place where many people go only at times when they want to remove the paper wrappings from candy bars and cough drops.

Concert pitch In the early history of music, pitch was not standardized. It varied from country to country, and even from city to city. This made life very difficult for musicians who want to travel (and you thought *time zones* were a problem...). Finally, after many attempts, a committee agreed in 1939 that pitch would be universally standardized and based upon A at 440 cycles per second. This made things much simpler for everyone, since now they all knew exactly what it was they were ignoring. Nowadays, A may be anywhere from about 425 to 450. Everyone agrees concert pitch is a marvelous idea.

Concerto A sort of musical boxing match between one musician (the soloist) and all the rest (the orchestra), with the conductor acting as referee, in which nobody wins — especially the audience.

Conductor The person at the front of the orchestra or choir, facing away from the audience (usually out of embarrassment). The musical conductor should not be confused with the railway conductor, who probably has more training (nor indeed with the electrical conductor, which probably has more spark). In music, the conductor's primary function is to imitate a windmill, for the esthetic effect. The conductor's chief weapon is

Conductor

the baton, which everyone is pretending to watch carefully. If the performance goes well, the conductor takes all the credit. If badly, the performers get the blame.

Console 1. (noun) The area of a church organ where the player sits, containing the keyboards, pedals, stops, pistons and other gizmos, including spare eyeglasses, those funny shoes organists need, throat lozenges, old paper clips and wadded-up tissues.

2. (verb) The act of comforting organists after they perform a piece badly: "Don't worry, it was the postlude. Nobody heard the wrong notes because they all left before you started playing anyway." And so on.

Consonants A subject of manic obsession among choirmasters. It's said that, by their use, one word may be distinguished from another. The origin of the myth is lost in the mists of Time and has never been successfully proven, since it's far beyond the capabilities of any singer.

Consumption 1. A disease that's supposed to affect operatic sopranos in the role of Mimi (in Puccini's *La Boheme*). The audience is forced to accept that a 200-pound woman who sings for four hours is wasting away. Yeah, right.

2. The act of reverence that unites musicians and alcohol in large quantities.

Contralto The second-highest vocal line sung by women (See Counter-tenor), lower than soprano or mezzo-soprano, but (usually) higher than male tenors. Generally has more brains and fewer annoying mannerisms than any of the above singers, though sometimes has a tendency to sound muffled and thick, as though she were singing with a pillow over her face or a mouthful of peanut butter. Contraltos have a tendency to sing flat and to sound like old molasses pudding. Derived from the Latin *altus*, which means "high" but which originally meant "overfed." In opera and other works, the contralto sometimes gets to play the villainess, but more often gets stuck with such roles as Old Wise Woman, Mysterious Countess, Earth Mother and so on.

Copyist A person hired by composers to transcribe pages of their illegible notation into other pages of the copyist's own notation, equally illegible.

Counterpoint

Counterpoint A musical device similar to needlepoint, although not designed to be hung on the wall or used on seat covers. Said to be a musical conversation, it more often resembles an argument. A favorite device of many Baroque composers, all of whom are now dead — although a direct connection between these two facts has never been conclusively established. Although no longer in practice by modern composers, it's still taught in schools, as a form of punishment.

Counter-tenor The highest adult male voice currently available through legal and moral means. Sings roughly (and roughly sings) the same range as the contralto, although he can sing lower if pressed, and higher if pinched. Counter-tenors have a tendency to sing on pitch, but out of rhythm, and to sound like a cross between an oboe and a buzzsaw. Derived from the Latin *contra tenore*, which means "against tenors." Without having to resort to radical surgery, counter-tenors are now sometimes used to re-create the *castrati* roles of Baroque operas. It's not entirely the same, but until someone is prepared to make the ultimate sacrifice of his personal life for the sake of art, it's about as close as we're going to get.

Counter-tenor

Critic Most critics are themselves frustrated musicians who now bear a continual grudge against their more successful (?) colleagues. They are usually employed by newspapers, and their job consists of attending a performance and then producing an instant written pronouncement on its quality. Because these articles are continually written under the pressure of deadlines, late at night after the performance when the critic would much rather be asleep comfortably in bed, reviews more often than not reflect an attitude of crankiness and bad temper. On the rare occasions that the critic writes a favorable review, the performers are so overjoyed that they forgive all the nasty things said in the past — at least until the next time the critic pans their performance.

Crook 1. A curved tube, part of a brass instrument, used for storing spit before its disposal onto the floor.
2. The type of person ideally suited for arts management.

Cross relation An angry relative.

Crotchet The English term for a quarter-note. Singers who perform too many of them are said to become crotchety.

Cruda sorte 1. Isabella's aria at the opening of Rossini's *L'Italiana in Algeri*.
2. A term you might use to describe some of the tough guys on the production crew, or the jerks who hang around the stage door trying to pick up the musicians.

Crwth An ancient string instrument invented by the fiendish Welsh — and even harder to play than it is to pronounce or spell.

Cue 1. An indication, especially from the conductor, that shows a musician when to enter.
2. A long, tapered wooden stick found in pool halls, and often used by an unemployed musician who has missed too many of the other kind of cues over the years.

Cycle 1. In the music of Schubert, Schumann, Wolf and other German *lieder* lovers, a way of grouping songs together to tell a long and convoluted story.
2. A two-wheeled means of transportation useful for escaping from performances involving long, convoluted groups of songs.

D

Da capo aria A particular type of aria with a built-in repeat, most often found in oratorio, opera and excess. Much favored by vain singers — there is no other kind — who are thus assured of at least one encore. From the Italian for "the head." Singers who perform too many *da capo* arias are often said to have let fame go to their heads — hence the name. Choirs have been known to stand up in the middle, to the confusion of the audience, who applaud half-heartedly.

Da Ponte, Lorenzo An Italian writer chiefly remembered for librettos to Mozart operas *Le nozze di Figaro*, *Don Giovanni* and *Cosi fan tutte*. He later moved to New York and found a real job, as a grocer.

Daughter of the Regiment, The An opera by Donizetti about a good-time party girl. The X-rated film version has yet to be released.

D.C. The abbreviation for *da capo* (Italian for "the head"), indicating a return to the start of a piece of music. Compare the indication Washington, D.C., so named because that's where the heads of the U.S. government reside.

Degree A term for the steps of a scale — or for the piece of paper from the school at which you learned your scales in the first place.

Diction That part of a singer's performance you can compliment when everything else is horrible. What most people really mean when they say diction is enunciation. Diction means the words chosen; enunciation means the clarity of their utterance. There's no sense complimenting singers on their diction, since the singers had nothing to do with writing the text. Trying to maintain this distinction, however, is a fruitless activity.

Dido's Lament The famous soprano aria from the closing death scene of Purcell's *Dido and Aeneas*. The text begins "When I am laid in earth ..." Easily misconstrued by those who think it begins only "When I am laid" — which has a different meaning entirely.

Diminished In harmonic terminology, the term to describe an interval that's been reduced by a small step. In financial terminology, the term to describe a musician's income after taxes.

Discord 1. Not to be confused with datchord.
2. The emotional state that usually exists among a group of musicians, especially with regard to those in authority.

Diva A fancy term for singer, especially the most important soprano(s) of a company — a matter of opinion (and fierce rivalry), of course. From the Italian for "goddess" — which unfortunately most of them take literally.

Dominant 1. In harmonic theory, the fifth degree of the scale.
2. A personality type important for musicians, and even more important for the conductor who must control them.
3. What parents must be if they expect their small children to practise for music lessons.

Don A popular Italian first name (see Don Carlos, Don Giovanni, Don Ottavio, and so on).

Dons

Double action The pianist's term for a *ménage à trois*.

Double-bass *(Editor's note: The information contained in this entry is unavailable, due to an injunction against the author successfully obtained by the Society for the Prevention of Cruelty to Double-Basses and the People Who Play Them. The legal battles continue, but it is the editor's hope that subsequent editions of this dictionary will be able to include this information in full.)*

Drums A percussion instrument originally played on the battlefield to inspire the troops and frighten the enemy. Even in modern times drums retain their military connotations, being chiefly played by teenagers who wish to frighten their parents or by those wanting to do battle with the neighbors.

Duet A performance for two musicians. Not to be confused with duel, which it often resembles.

I play, old boy!

The English horn

E

Ear An external auditory organ essential for hearing. Often present but sadly non-functional on many musicians.

Early music In classical music, anything before about 1600. In rock music, anything before about noon.

Embellishment 1. A musical term for notes that are fancy addition(s) to an otherwise plain tune.

2. A cynical term for musicians who are fancy addition(s) to an otherwise plain group.

Encore A nasty method by which performers get back at the audience for its feigned appreciation in the form of applause. It consists of performing an extra piece "off the cuff" (which has been slavishly prepared for weeks). Audiences would be well advised not to applaud at all, so everyone can get home that much sooner.

End-plugged The term for an organ pipe stopped at one end, which lowers its pitch by an octave. The term is sometimes also applied to organists themselves, because their cranky, distracted disposition is often the result of chronic constipation from sitting too long on organ benches.

English horn A woodwind instrument so named because it's neither English nor a horn. Not to be confused with the French horn, which is German.

Ensemble 1. Any group of individual performers who are supposed to function as a unit.
2. The feeling of co-operation and togetherness that such groups lack.

Enunciation What most people really mean when they use to the term diction (see Diction).

Envelope In electronic music, the term used to describe the growth and decay of a note or sound. In financial terms, the object containing a payment that determines the growth or decay of a musician's bank balance.

Execution 1. A term used to describe the act of performing music: "I think the performer's execution of that phrase was marvelous."
2. A technique for dealing with musicians who fail in the above endeavor: "I think the performer's execution

would be a good idea — preferably by firing squad."

Exercise A short activity — such as scales, arpeggios, small pieces — meant to improve a performer's technique by means of constant repetition. Also, any repetitive physical activity most usefully practised by overweight musicians.

Exposition In a fugue, the exposition is the musical equivalent of having wallpaper that matches the furniture.

Expression 1. An indication in the score conveying information about tempo, dynamics, articulation or other means of shaping a musical phrase.
2. The pained look on the conductor's face when the performers ignore such indications.

F

Falsetto A vocal technique used by men to achieve notes in the highest range. Less permanent — and less painful — than that used for the *castrato* sound. The product of dedication, discipline, muscular control — or sometimes stepping the wrong way on a garden rake.

Fancy The term applied in the 16th century to certain light-hearted musical works and in later centuries to certain performers and the way they dress.

Fantasy What most musicians have instead of a sex life.

False relation The kind of relative supportive of your musical career only if you're making money.

Farinelli The stage name for Carlo Broschi, one of the greatest of the Italian *castrati* of the 18th century. After operatic triumphs in Italy and England, he retired early to the court of the King of Spain, where he relaxed playing harpsichord, collecting fine paintings and running the Madrid opera house — having nothing much better to do with his time.

 **Fedora** 1. A fancy opera written in 1898 by Umberto Giordano.

 2. A fancy hat worn around the same time by Giuseppe Verdi.

Fermata A pause in the music, useful as a sort of rallying point for getting back together if things are falling apart. Composers are well advised to include several, judiciously spaced throughout the score.

Fiddle 1. A slang term for violin.
2. A slang term for what many unscrupulous impresarios do to the concert hall books.

Fidelio Beethoven's famous opera about prison reform and marital fidelity — themes that have proven to be less than stellar draws at the box office (which may explain why it's Beethoven's only opera). The only opera in the repertoire with four overtures, three of them named *Leonore Overtures*, just to confuse matters. See the entry under Leonore, which might help explain things. Or it might not.

Fifth A convenient quantity of alcohol to be consumed before, during or after a performance (see Bar).

Figaro, The Marriage of A popular comic opera by Mozart. Confusingly, does *not* contain the famous aria *Figaro, Figaro, Figaro*. Some people refuse to believe this, and no amount of explaining will convince them otherwise.

Figure 1. A small and recognizable grouping of notes.
2. The aspect of a musician's appearance that expands with time. (See Pasta.)

Fitzwilliam Virginal Book The famous book belonging to a notorious 16th-century rake, cad and womanizer named Thomas William Orlando Fitzwilliam, who was said to enjoy a challenge. It contains a list of the most desirable and innocent young ladies of Elizabethan London. Fitzwilliam died of old age and exhaustion, the day after his 23rd birthday.

Flageolet A small end-blown flute used in early music

*The Marriage
of Figaro*

and nowadays for performing Irish jigs and reels. Not to be confused with flagellate, the whipping we'd like to give some players after having to listen to too many jigs and reels.

Flat An adjective used to describe a tone that's slightly below pitch. This term ought to be used cautiously, so as not to offend anyone, especially when applied to a woman.

Flats Little marks that look like this: ♭ and that resemble small b's that have been deflated, or sat upon. They're similar to sharps, but different. Their function is to lower a note by a semitone (more or less). When gathered together at the beginning of a line, they form a key signature. This means that each corresponding note should be lowered by a semitone whenever it occurs, or whenever the performer remembers to do so. The double-flat lowers the note by two semitones, or one whole tone. This latter confusing distinction was invented solely to provide work for theorists and publishers.

Florid 1. The musical term for a passage with lots of extra notes.
2. The medical term for a musician's complexion after performing such a passage.

Flute A sophisticated peashooter with a range up to 500 yards and deadly accuracy in close quarters. Blown transversely to confuse the enemy, it can be dismantled into three small pieces, for easy concealment.

Form 1. The shape of a composition.
2. The shape of the musician who plays the composition.
3. The piece of paper that must be completed in triplicate (known as ternary form) for the musician to get enough money from the arts council to play the composition.

How flats are made

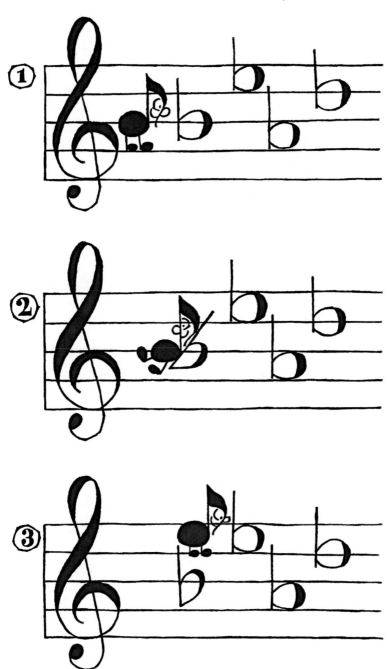

French horn A brass instrument that resembles a snail, but sometimes moves more quickly. The complicated instrument of today is a direct descendant of the early horn used by hunters. It was originally long and straight, but got its present shape when trod upon by a horse. The French horn is actually German, and should not be confused with the English horn, which is French.

Fret 1. In guitars and other stringed instruments, small pieces of metal across the neck that make tuning easier. 2. Among singers, the backstage activity akin to panic that results from realizing no such devices exist to make the singer's tuning easier.

Fugue A type of Baroque composition similar to a crossword puzzle, but with fewer clues. The greatest fugue composer was J.S. Bach, who died before completing his seminal work, *The Art of Fugue.* Many musicians since have died trying to play it. (One misguided musicologist who thought Fugue was actually an 18th-century portrait painter was unceremoniously drummed out of the profession, and has since made a fortune writing record-liner notes.)

Fuguing tune 1. A type of simple, repetitive melody popular in 18th-century America. 2. In the music of Wagner, Lloyd Webber, the minimalists and others, an expression often heard when a simple, repetitive melody keeps coming back and won't go away, as in: "Do we have to listen to this fuguing tune again?!"

Fundamental discord 1. In harmony, the name for a chord in which the discordant note is an essential element (for example, the seventh in a dominant-seventh chord) and not just a passing note or a mistake. 2. The emotional state in which most musicians operate.

Glissando

G

Gapped The term for a musical scale or melody with notes missing, or the smile of some performers with teeth missing. (Especially true of trumpet players in marching bands who don't watch where they're going.)

Gay, John An English poet and playwright of the 18th century, best remembered for providing the libretto to *The Beggar's Opera* in 1728. He warmed up for the job by writing the libretto for *Acis and Galatea*, by Handel, from whom *The Beggar's Opera* later stole some of its best tunes.

Gig The musician's slang term for a job or performance. Not to be confused with gigue, a type of happy dance often performed by musicians who've just landed a gig.

Glissando The musical equivalent of stepping on a banana peel. Performed by some musicians in the theory that one of the notes along the way is bound to be right.

Gopak See Hopak.

Götterdämmerung 1. An opera by Wagner, the fourth and last in the *Ring* cycle.
2. An expression often heard from the audience of Wagner operas. (As in, "Isn't this *götterdämmerung* opera finished yet?")

Grace note Every once in a while, the solo performer will attempt an interval, jumping from one note to another. In many instances, this is mere guesswork. If the wrong note is landed on, the performer may attempt to slide up or down to the correct one. The resulting confusion is politely called a grace note. A surprising term, since in many such instances, very little gracefulness is involved.

Grand A term variously applied to a type of opera, a type of piano, a large musical staff or the thousand bucks you might earn for playing any one of them.

Grand opera The general term for serious operas, in which people die at the end. Distinguished from Comic opera, in which people get married at the end. In other words, one has a happy ending, the other a sad ending. You get to decide which is which.

Grave An Italian term meaning "slow" or "solemn." Appropriately enough, it's often found as a tempo indication in funeral music.

Gregorian chant A type of unison singing invented by monks as a mask for snoring.

Groves, Sir George Only one of many persons who may be turning over in their graves at this point.

Guerre des Bouffons The so-called "War of the Buffoons," an argument among the Paris elite of 1752 between supporters of the old-fashioned Italian style and newer French style of Rameau and others. Sparked by a revival performance of Pergolesi's *La serva padrona*, possibly just as a means of keeping it in the history books. The tradition survives today, in which buffoons continue to argue about opera.

A Grand opera curtain call

H

Handel, G.F. A German-born English Baroque composer of music in all genres, including the famous oratorio *Messiah* and such operas as *Acis and Galatea, Giulio Cesare, Rinaldo, Serse* and many others. Handel later abandoned operas when he found he couldn't earn a living composing them — a pragmatic example that many others would do well to follow.

Harmony A sort of musical sociology. The study of the inter-relationship of individual notes and how they react in group encounters, such as tone clusters and orgies. Theorists and others who study harmony have developed a highly intricate system of confusing terminology, to disguise the fact that they really don't know what's going on. The aspiring student of harmony should practise saying phrases such as "secondary sub-mediant appoggiatura six-four" or "first-inversion Neapolitan five-seven of five, sharp four plus eleven, going to a half-diminished seven of six" until they sound convincing. If unable to do this in a convincing manner, you may be in the wrong profession, or ought at least to consider becoming a critic, where even the most rudimentary knowledge of music isn't needed. It may, in fact, be a hindrance.

Harpsichord A type of keyboard instrument, a precursor of the piano, and cursed at ever since. Sir Thomas Beecham described its sound as that of "two skeletons copulating on a corrugated tin roof."

Head 1. In singers, a term used to describe a particularly

light and floating vocal tone.
2. In opera singers especially, the large and empty space above the neck that provides extra resonance.

Heel The bottom end of the bow used by violinists, cellists and other players of bowed string instruments. By extension, then, the term is also often applied to the players themselves (see Bent, Nut).

Heldentenor The German term for "heroic tenor," found in operas of Wagner and others, suitable for singers with bigger voices and even smaller brains than usual.

Hell 1. A place of unending agony, torture and suffering often used as an operatic plot device (in *Don Giovanni, Faust, Orpheus in the Underworld* and many others) and referenced in the text of many Requiem masses.
2. Anything by Wagner.

Hemiola A rhythmic device similar to a hernia.

Hidden fifths 1. In the strict rules of harmony and counterpoint, a stylistic error much deplored by pedantic professors.
2. A method by which many overstressed musicians, driven to drink (often by obscure and unreasonable rules of harmony and counterpoint imposed by their pedantic professors), help to calm their frazzled nerves.

Hopak See Gopak.

I

Idyll 1. A pleasant period of gentle peace and enjoyment. Not to be confused with the serial music of Schönberg or the operas of Wagner, for instance, which is pretty much the exact opposite. 2. In music, a short composition meant to portray such an event. Among the best known — and most surprising — of these is Wagner's *Siegfried Idyll*, which includes themes from that opera.

Imbroglio 1. In opera, the Italian term for a section of complicated music meant to suggest scheming, manipulation and confusion. 2. In most musical organizations, the general state of affairs.

Imitation The sincerest form of counterpoint.

Impresario The person who arranges all the details of presenting an opera or other musical production, in the hopes of impressing people. Possibly also related to the term imprecise, which describes the impresario's chance of actually predicting a production's success.

Inflection 1. In plainchant, the term for those sections, especially at the beginning and end, more elaborate than the usual boring monotone bits. 2. A term for sharps, flats and other indications that raise or lower notes by a semitone or more. Not to be confused with infection, a virus prone to afflicting singers that often raises their temperature while lowering their vocal range by a semitone or more.

Instrument That object by which many musicians make noise and earn their livelihoods. To a certain extent, a player can improve merely by replacing an old instrument by a better one (or, strangely with violins and other strings, a new instrument by an older one). This never happens as often as it should. Instruments, like their players, come in various shapes and sizes, and various degrees of unpleasantness.

Interval 1. The distance, real or imagined, between two notes.
2. The British term for intermission — the break that gives performers a chance to go to the bathroom, and the audience a chance to sneak out early.
3. The waiting period between a performer's previous entry and the next. May vary from one bar to forever.

Interval

Invention 1. A short imitative work for two or three voices, much favored by J.S. Bach.
2. A facility other musicians might find useful, especially when preparing expense accounts or income-tax statements.

Iphegenia In ancient Greek legend, a young woman with a lousy sense of direction (see *Iphegenia in Aulis*, *Iphegenia in Tauris* and so on).

Italy The cradle of the opera tradition, and the country still largely responsible for keeping it alive. All blame, complaints, class-action suits and other legal proceedings should be directed there.

J

Jam 1. A session at which jazz musicians improvise, usually late at night.
2. A sweet confection they spread on their toast the next morning.

Jaw A portion of the human facial anatomy useful to singers and other musicians especially for articulation, forming the embouchure, enumerating contract demands — and breaking (better it be someone else's) when those contract demands are not met.

Jazz A style of music occasionally found in (for example, *Porgy and Bess*), and in any case infinitely superior to, the standard opera repertoire.

Jewels Articles of adornment often worn by musicians both on stage and off. Although many of them may be precious family heirlooms, these should not be confused with family jewels, which in the case of the *castrati* have been removed.

Joint 1. Especially in jazz or rock, musicians' slang for a bar, club or other venue where a performance takes place.
2. Also especially in jazz or rock, musicians' slang for the funny cigarette often consumed in such venues.

K

Kettledrums Despite their name, these drums aren't very useful for making coffee or tea, since they're far too large and would take too long to boil the water. This is regrettable, since they aren't much use for anything else. Several composers in the past have used kettledrums to imitate sounds of battle and of rumbling thunder. Nowadays, they're used increasingly to imitate certain of the grosser bodily functions. Other than that, percussionists find them useful tables for chessboards.

Key 1. Certain musical terms defy easy definition. This is one of them.
2. A device for opening doors at an opera house or concert hall (not to be confused with bribe).

Key signature As explained above (see Flats), a key signature is the attempt to organize what would otherwise be an unruly mob of accidentals into some sort of order at the beginning of each line of the staff. These sharps or flats (but rarely both) may number from none to seven, and their order and placement on the staff are rigidly controlled by music publishers, who are now too lazy to change their established typesetting. Several mnemonic phrases exist to help the musician remember the proper order of accidentals, the most useful being "Father Christmas gets diarrhea after eating biscuits" for the flats (or is it the sharps?) and — actually I can't remember the other one.

Keyboard A type of instrument (piano, harpsichord and

so on), used to accompany performances, especially in rehearsal. Not to be confused with key bored, a sign the composer should consider a modulation.

Klavierstück A term used by German furniture movers trying to get a piano through a narrow doorway.

Kettledrum

L

Lablache, Luigi A famous 19th-century Italian bass, celebrated for performances as Leporello in Mozart's *Don Giovanni*, the title role in Donizetti's *Don Pasquale* and many others. Sang at the funerals of Haydn, Beethoven and Chopin. Maybe he was a jinx.

La donna è mobile The well-known tenor aria from Verdi's *Rigoletto* in which the Duke of Mantua relates his attitude toward women. Roughly translated from the Italian (well, very roughly), the phrase means: "Boy, look at that woman move!"

Largo al factotum Figaro's famous patter song from the opening of Rossini's *Barber of Seville* in which he lists his many duties and responsibilities. Seen by many as an early form of labor-relations contract, though considered less binding in a court of law.

Largo, Handel's The popular name given to instrumental arrangements of a famous aria from Handel's opera *Serse*. The term is inaccurate, since the passage itself is actually marked Larghetto, which is still slow, but a little faster than Largo. (But somehow Handel's *Larghetto* just doesn't have the right ring to it.) In the opera, the aria, *Ombra mai fù*, is the hero's passionate address to a big tree — which may explain why it so often gets such a wooden performance.

Laryngitis The second-most effective and convincing way to silence a singer. The most effective way is death — though somewhat drastic, perhaps. It's only

one of a large number of similar afflictions — such as the flu, colds, strep throat and *delirium tremens* — all of which have been known to affect singers at the least-opportune times. Such catastrophes are extremely prevalent among soloists, and have been known to lay waste to entire choirs at Christmas time. Depending on your perspective, it may be seen as either a curse or a blessing — maybe even a form of divine retribution.

Lay-clerk This term, used to describe certain types of singers in English cathedral and college choirs, is actually not as rude as it may appear.

Leer 1. A musical term from the German for "empty." It can refer to open strings of the violin or similar instruments and sometimes to the intellectual capacity (or bank accounts) of musicians.
2. The look one musician will sometimes give another. Often followed by a slap or rude remark.

Leitmotiv From the German for "leading motif," a fancy, highbrow term to describe recurring little signature tunes that in opera may be associated with a particular character, object, idea or place. The 19th-century equivalent of today's radio and TV commercial jingles, though neither as clever nor entertaining. Often misspelled *"leitmotif,"* a piece of information useful for detecting and deflating pretentious musical snobs (there is no other kind). Mozart, Weber, Berlioz and other composers have used *leitmotivs*, but the practice is most often associated with Wagner — who in the *Ring* cycle went a little nuts on the subject, actually. (It was a short trip.) For reasons no one quite understands, Wagner preferred the term *hauptmotiv*, but history has overruled him on the issue. (Unfortunately, it wasn't able to overrule him on many others.)

Leonore The heroine of Beethoven's only opera, and one of the few happily and faithfully married characters in the entire operatic repertoire. Beethoven wrote four *Leonore* overtures, all of them for an opera he then called *Fidelio*. Go figure. The fourth is now generally the one played to start the opera and so is called the *Fidelio Overture*. *Leonore No. 3* is often performed to introduce the final act. *Leonores 1* and *2* didn't make the cut.

Leporello The faithful servant (bass) to the hero in Mozart's *Don Giovanni*. He sings the famous *Catalogue Aria* (*Madamina! il catalogo è questo*) in the opening scene, bragging about the number of his boss's romantic conquests. (This was long before political correctness. Nowadays his account would be considered part of a victim impact statement.) Just for the record, Leporello lists 640 in Italy, 231 in Germany, an even 100 in France, a mere 91 in Turkey and an astounding 1,003 in Spain (where Don Giovanni obviously had the home-court advantage), for a grand total of 2,065. But considering the number Don Giovanni actually succeeds with in his own opera (i.e. zilch), it's probably fair to assume Leporello is exaggerating just a bit — basking in his master's reflected glory, obviously. Or just sucking up to the boss.

Libiamo The famous drinking song in the opening act of Verdi's *La Traviata*. An instance of officially sanctioned drinking on stage — as opposed to the drinking in most other operas, which takes place off in the wings or the dressing rooms.

Libretto In opera or oratorio, the term for the lyrics and dialogue that make up the story. From the Italian for "little book," a useful reminder to the prudent audience member to bring along a good book to read in case the performance itself is a deadly bore.

Lohengrin A famous Wagner opera about a bunch of heroic knights. Possibly based on a much earlier work, later discarded — *Low 'n' Green,* about a bunch of heroic frogs.

Lothario 1. In Thomas's opera *Mignon,* a wandering old minstrel who turns out to be a nobleman.
2. In other operas in general, any old musician with wandering hands who turns out to be far from noble.

Lust 1. The German word for "light," as in the prisoners' chorus *O Welche Lust,* from Beethoven's opera, *Fidelio.*
2. The sort of feeling likely to interfere with a musician's practice time, not to mention good judgment (see Passion, Rhapsody).

Lute A string instrument of the Medieval and Renaissance periods, resembling a bloated guitar. It was frequently used to provide background music at mealtimes. It can have as many as 16 sets of strings (most of them in pairs), which are referred to as "courses." (With 16 courses at mealtime, no wonder it was bloated.) It gets its name from the Arabic *el oude,* the meaning of which has, until recently, eluded musicologists — who are the only ones who would care, anyway. It's now known that the name comes from the practice of using this instrument to accompany lewd songs.

Mad scene

M

Madrigal A type of part-song, popular in the Renaissance, for unaccompanied voices. Often involves one of the earliest examples of censorship in music: Some of the refrains were so lewd and suggestive they had to be replaced by repetitions of "fa-la-la." (Pedantic music-ologists — there is no other kind — may at this point mention that the proper term for such a madrigal is "ballett." Humor them and they may go away.)

Mad scene A common operatic plot device that allows singers (usually sopranos) to display elaborate vocal technique, dramatic skill and their true personality type. Found in such operas as Berg's *Lulu* and Donizetti's *Anna Bolena* and *Lucia di Lammermoor*. Also frequently found off stage when contracts are being renewed.

Mediation 1. In plainchant, a form of inflection at the end of the first section of a psalm (see Inflection, not to be confused with infection).
2. A form of legal negotiation sometimes resorted to among musicians when contract talks break down. Not to be confused with medication, the drugs the musicians might have to take to survive the mediation process.

Maestro An affectionate nickname (from the Italian "master") for the conductor of operas and other musical productions. Used in public and polite company, as opposed to the other nicknames often given to conductors — most of which are unprintable in a book aimed at general audiences.

Magic Flute, The Mozart's famous and popular opera about the triumph of true love over dangers that include a deadly dragon, a vengeful mother-in-law, mystical magic spells and one really loopy guy in a bird suit.

Mass 1. A term to describe the central religious ceremony of the Christian church, for which generations of composers have provided music.
2. A term to describe the overall bulk of singers and other musicians, which seems to increase as their careers progress. (See Pasta.)

Melba, Nellie An Australian coloratura soprano of the late 19th and early 20th centuries who became so popular she had not one but two food dishes named after her: Peach Melba and Melba toast. Appropriate symbolism, really, since singers whose careers aren't peachy just end up as toast.

Melody That aspect of music most often sacrificed to a musician's ego. (But see also Rhythm.)

Messiah An oratorio by Handel, attempted every Christmas by some choir that thinks it's good enough, and in collaboration with instrumentalists, who need the money. It's the musical equivalent of death and taxes: inescapable and excruciating.

Messiah

Mezza voce From the Italian for "half-voice," a technique of singing more quietly. In most opera singers, this reduces the tone from the ear-splitting to the merely uncomfortable.

Mezzo-soprano A sort of half-hearted (sometimes half-witted) soprano. Marginally more intelligent, due to the reduced effect of high notes, which addle the brain. With fewer high notes generally come fewer temper tantrums. In opera, sometimes plays the heroine but more often is just a sidekick.

Mime The term for a performer who remains entirely silent. In Wagner's *Ring* cycle, the name of one of the Nibelung dwarfs, the brother of Alberich and foster father of Siegfried. Operas in general, and Wagner's in particular, ought to have more mimes — at least the kind who shut up and don't sing.

Mixture 1. For organs, the blending of certain pipes to obtain a more pleasing sound.
2. For organists, the blending of certain alcoholic ingredients to obtain a more pleasing beverage, or to drown out the sound of certain organ pipes.

Modern music The name given in polite company to the mess we're in now. Often used when people don't know what else to call it. (See Noise.) It's important to remember that musical styles are rarely popular when they're new and current, and rarely unpopular when they're old and established. The music of Beethoven, for example, was considered far too "modern" when he wrote it. But of course nowadays the music of Beethoven is considered wonderful and great. It's a frightening prospect to consider that the same may be said of today's music, a hundred years from now.

Modes Groups into which notes were organized before the invention of scales, the introduction of which caused them to become outmoded.

Modulation A means of getting from one key to another,

similar to changing lanes on the highway, and just as hazardous if done recklessly. Unsuccessful modulations may lead to atonality — a sort of 12-car pileup.

Monody A compositional style for single voice and accompaniment developed in Italy in the early 16th century by Caccini and members of the Florentine Camerata. An early stage in the development of opera. Not to be confused with monotony, which comes in the later stages.

Monteverdi, Claudio An influential and prolific Italian composer (1567-1643) considered by many (except friends and family of Caccini, Peri and that crowd) to be the "father" of opera. Any class-action (or paternity) suits should be directed to the Monteverdi estate.

DEAR OLD DAD

Motives 1. The plural of *motiv* (sometimes *motif*), the name for a short melodic phrase or fragment used by composers to establish thematic material. Often called melodic motives.
2. Impulses that drive musicians to certain, usually selfish, behaviors. Often called ulterior motives.

Mozart, Wolfgang Amadeus Child prodigy and musical genius of the 18th century (1756-91), put on Earth as God's way of making the rest of us feel insignificant. A superb composer in all forms and genres, even his operas — *The Magic Flute, The Marriage of Figaro, Don Giovanni* and others — are wonderful and good fun, too (just to prove it can work when it's done right).

Muse In ancient Greek myth, one of several beautiful

women who took credit for inspiring poets, musicians and other creative types — but who, unfortunately, never stuck around to take the blame if their inspirations didn't work out. In this respect, they are the forerunners of the modern-day artistic directors who get fired or jump ship between seasons, so they don't have to stick around to see their elaborate and unworkable plans fall to ruins.

Music 1. Any combination of sounds and words, akin to noise and cacophony, produced (intentionally or by accident) by musicians (also, though rarely, by singers). 2. The printed form of obscure hieroglyphics, squiggles, scrawls and blots that purport to tell the musician how to produce the desired noise. It may be (a) illegible, (b) boring, (c) too difficult, or (d) any combination thereof. The production of music follows three stages. It is:
1. set down by the composer
2. Interpreted (incorrectly) by the conductor and
3. Ignored by the performers and audience.

Music drama A term often used throughout history in place of opera (in Italian, *dramma per musica*), and the term preferred by Wagner to describe the mammoth, bloated spectacles he inflicted on his unsuspecting audiences. (Although you'd think, after the first one, they'd have started to catch on.)

Music lesson A form of cruel and unusual punishment inflicted on young children by their parents and on teachers by their shrinking bank balances. In such instances, it's a debatable point which is more unbalanced — the bank account or the music teacher.

Music stand An intricate device for propping up music, except at crucial times — such as during the performance. It has a tendency to fall over, often of its own accord. It comes in two sizes — too high or too low — and is always broken.

Musica ficta Ancient rules for the interpretation of early music. A sort of musical *Everyday Etiquette*. In Medieval times, the principles of *ficta* were understood by everybody, so they were never written down. Nowadays, nobody can write them down, because nobody understands them at all.

Musical 1. The adjective pertaining to music, used to describe a state or quality that embodies music.
2. In modern theatre, the term to describe the popular successor of the operatic form, a production on Broadway or elsewhere that includes singers, dancers and instrumentalists in a comic or dramatic story told in music. The most successful composer of the modern musical is Andrew Lloyd Webber, whose works include *Cats, Evita* and *Phantom of the Opera*.
3. In many such Broadway-style shows, the essential quality some productions lack. Ironically, many musicals are hardly musical at all.

Musicians Individuals bent upon producing sound or noise by means of scraping, hitting, beating or blowing into an object made of wood, brass or catgut. In a performance, each may be seen wearing an ill-fitting tuxedo or black dress. (In most cases, the men wear tuxedos and the women wear dresses.) Orchestral musicians are allowed to sit, for which they get paid extra. Choral musicians rarely get paid at all, and they must stand throughout the performance, unless they faint. Most musicians can count to at least four, and some to five. Not to be confused with singers.

Musicians' union A powerful branch of the Mafia that controls the exorbitant amounts of money paid to musicians, and also the number of coffee breaks permitted per hour (at least one, and usually three, with pay). Singers, not being musicians, aren't required to be members. All others must join, the penalty being blacklisting, or preferably death.

Mute A device for muffling the sound of certain instruments — notably the trumpet, trombone and violin — reducing their tone from excruciating to merely annoying. Unfortunately, efforts to design mutes for certain other instruments — the bagpipes and accordion spring immediately to mind — have been less successful.

Musician's union

N

Nabucco See Nebuchadnezzar.

Nadir 1. One of the pearl fishers, a tenor, in Bizet's opera *Les Pêcheurs de Perles*.
2. A scientific term to describe the lowest possible point, the bottom, the deepest pit in the ocean and so on.
3. In music, a term to describe the level of quality reached by some productions, or the place it might be best to put them.

Natural 1. In musical terminology, a note that has neither a flat nor sharp.
2. In opera, an adjective used to describe a style of performing (acting or singing) much admired and rarely obtained. (See Wooden.)

Nebuchadnezzar 1. An ancient Babylonian king, the title character of Verdi's opera *Nabucco* (the Italian spelling's easier).
2. A very large bottle of Champagne, larger than a magnum, suitable for consuming after an opera (especially Verdi).

Neck 1. The long, narrow part of many stringed instruments (violin, ukulele and others) that joins the pegboard to the soundbox.
2. The shorter, thicker part of many musicians suitable for wringing when they botch a performance (or just

on general principles).

Nibelungen A class of dwarfs known chiefly to inhabit the operas of Wagner, where they fashion magic rings and helmets, raise orphans and hang around damp caves. Despite extensive vocation counselling, no more productive occupation has yet been found for them.

Node 1. The point of rest between two portions of a vibrating string.
2. A sign of strain that sometimes afflicts singers who have injured their vocal cords.
3. In less severe cases, that portion of a singer's facial anatomy that gets all stuffy during a bad cold or nasal infection. (Among singers, this is known as having "a code in de node.")

Noise A more accurate term for sound. In general, noise is considered to be disorganized sound — as opposed to music, which is organized sound. Sometimes, especially in opera (see Wagner), it's hard to tell the difference. In some modern music, there is no difference.

None 1. In Gregorian tradition, one of several liturgical services held throughout the day, this one "at the ninth hour" — that is, three o'clock in the morning.
2. The number of listeners likely to show up at any such service held at three o'clock in the morning.

Notes Little black dots with stems and flags that are the peculiar language of music. The "whole" note is divided into "halves," "quarters" and so on. These divisions are usually referred to as "long," "short" and "really short." Widely held to be understood by musicians (and sometimes by singers), they are, in fact, a bafflement to all — but everyone is too proud to admit it. Although in theory such notation is actually quite precise, in practice the two events — notation and performance — are often miles apart. (In the case of

Canadian or European performances, kilometres.) In each case there is a great matter of pride involved. Composers take pride in notating their ideas as accurately as possible, and performers take pride in ignoring them as "artistically" as possible.

2. Notes are also reminders of interpretation, performance practice, stage direction and so on that a director or conductor will give to performers during rehearsals. These are likewise ignored.

Nuance A degree of subtlety (in interpretation, gesture, performance) entirely beyond the capabilities of many performers, and indeed of many composers.

Nut The narrow ridge across the neck of a string instrument such as the violin, situated near the pegbox. By extension, then, the term has come to be applied to any person who plays such an instrument (see Bent, Heel).

Opera buffa

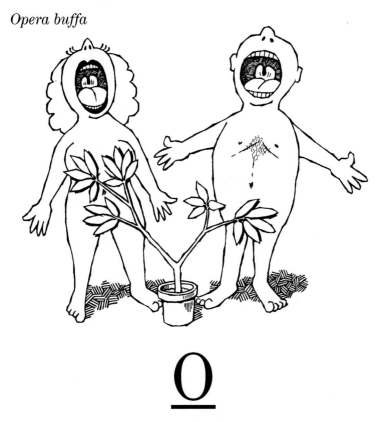

O

Obbligato The fancy Italian term composers use to designate that a certain instrument must be used in a particular passage. The musical equivalent of a binding contract. Interestingly, the term is rarely if ever applied to specific singing voices. (Composers may be demanding, but they're not stupid.)

Oboe (trad.) An ill wind that nobody blows good.

Octave A distance of approximately eight notes (12 if it includes all semitones, as many as 27 if sung by a tenor).

Opera A performance involving singers with orchestra (complete with unrealistic scenery and silly costumes), which tells a story so complex that nobody in the audience understands what's going on, although all speak about it as if they did. Consists mainly of fat people bellowing in a foreign language. In other words, an overrated production in which overweight performers sing overblown music in overpriced theatres for overlong periods of time. Actually, the stereotype that all opera singers are fat, stupid and arrogant is hardly fair. Some of them have lost weight recently.

Opera buffa Not, as you might expect, opera in the nude. Not yet, anyway. Not to be confused with opera buffet, a little party that comes after the performance.

Opera lover A person who believes that nothing succeeds like excess.

Operetta A less serious or pretentious form of opera designed for popular entertainment. A kind of calorie-reduced Opera Lite, with less fat and generally easier to digest.

Orchestra The result of musicians' having discovered there's safety in numbers. So much so that the orchestra often outnumbers its audience. Can be distinguished from a mob only by the fact that a mob chooses weapons such as placards and stones, while an orchestra chooses weapons such as violins and trumpets. Also, mobs rarely wear tuxedos.

Orchestra pit 1. A deep hole, in the front of and below the stage, where the orchestra performs and into which things (including persons) have a tendency to fall.
2. (Doubtful) That part of an orchestra left over when one has digested all of the rest, and which ought to be spat into the garbage (cf. cherries, peaches, avocados, etc.) or planted. Science has, as yet, been unable to cultivate an orchestra by this method, although some of its failures are no worse than many orchestras already in existence.

Orchestra pit

Orfeo A character from Greek myth, husband of Euridice, and a central role in several operas, including the earliest by Peri and Monteverdi, and later ones by Gluck, Offenbach and others. A musician and a bit of a whiner, actually, and prone to wandering around the nether regions without many clothes on, except on his own nether regions (see Offenbach's *Orpheus in his Underwear*). Not to be confused with Oreo, which is a kind of cookie.

Organ A mythical instrument, part man and part beast, known to inhabit churches — especially ones that are cold, damp, drafty and impoverished. In constant need of repairs and impossible to tune, it has a very large range: The highest notes attract bats and the lowest loosen the floorboards. Everything in between sounds like a cross between thunderous cisterns and cold porridge. Most often used to accompany choirs, and to provide background noise for the church service. It can also be an effective means of suppressing sermons.

Organist The person hired by a church to play the organ and to provide music for services, weddings, funerals and other joyous occasions. Not to be confused with the organ student, who actually does the playing.

Organ student A species of sub-organist, or a sub-species of organist.

Orlofsky, Prince A "pants role" in Johann Strauss's *Die Fledermaus*, usually sung by a mezzo, the kind who nowadays might appear on an afternoon talk show. ("Women who dress up like men and crash parties." "I'm a mezzo trapped in a baritone's body." "My husband lets me wear the pants in the family.") See Travesti.

Ornamentation 1. The practice of adding extra notes to a melody in order to improve it, or to disguise one's inability to perform it properly. The fancy bits that dress up an otherwise plain piece of music.
2. The only reason some persons are allowed to remain in a musical organization. The fancy bits who dress up an otherwise plain chorus line or orchestra.

Overblown 1. In wind instruments, a term to describe notes higher than should normally be produced.
2. An excessively elaborate performance or production, often one involving notes (and salaries) higher than should normally be produced.

Overtures 1. Instrumental pieces that introduce operas,

oratorios and other musical forms.
2. Romantic advances that introduce musicians to each other.

Ornamentation

P

Pagliacci, I The famous tragic opera by Leoncavallo with a bunch of clowns on stage. Or rather, the famous opera in which all the clowns on stage are actually meant to be clowns.

Pang 1. A tenor role in Puccini's *Turandot*.
2. A kind of stomach pain suffered by singers, often those attempting Puccini tenor roles.

Pants role See Travesti.

Papagena and Papageno Silly young lovers in Mozart's *The Magic Flute* — the Mutt and Jeff, Frick and Frack, Burns and Allen, Bill and Ted, Harold and Kumar of the operatic world.

Parlando In opera, a style of singing that's closer to speaking — as opposed to the usual style, which is closer to screaming.

Parsifal The hero and title character of one of Wagner's operas, a noble medieval knight sent on a sacred Grail quest and described in the story as a "guileless fool." It's a tenor role, obviously.

Partial 1. In the study of acoustics, a term to describe each multiple of a fundamental vibration.
2. In musical productions, a term to describe the biased attitude of the conductor or artistic director.
3. In some musicians a term to describe that portion of

brain capacity they are capable of using (also known as negligible).

Passion 1. A highly emotional state often required by composers on stage and demonstrated by performers off stage.

2. One of any number of long-winded oratorios by Bach or others, telling the death and resurrection of Christ. Usually told in the version according to one of the four Gospels. (*The Passion According to the Reuters Jerusalem Correspondent* has not received the attention it deserves.) The performance is ideally suited to the Easter season, since at the end the audience has the feeling of having eaten too many Easter eggs and the performers feel as if they've laid one.

3. The sort of feeling that's apt to interfere with a musician's practice time, not to mention meals (see Lust, Rhapsody).

Pasta, Giuditta An Italian operatic soprano of the early 19th century, celebrated for creating such roles as Bellini's *Norma* and *La Sonnambula* and Donizetti's *Anna Bolena*. In her honor, opera singers consume enormous amounts of pasta each year.

Perfect Fool, The 1. A one-act opera by Gustav Holst, first performed in 1923.

2. A name for anyone who willingly attends an opera performance, especially of Wagner.

Pedal-point Not to be confused with counterpoint or needlepoint. A compositional device, used especially in pieces for the organ (which badly need it), by which the listener is forewarned that the end is near (of the music, that is). It consists of a long-held note in the bass, sometimes the result of the organist's foot having gone to sleep.

Pedals A special keyboard on the organ, operated by the player's feet, used for the lowest bass notes. Unlike bicycles and tricycles, which also have pedals, there's little to be gained — and much to be lost — by pedalling the organ as fast as you can.

Pencil This small object is what distinguishes the professional musician from the mere amateur. No self-respecting musician should be without one, and the union imposes heavy fines on anyone unable to produce one, like a union card, on demand. For this reason, pencils should be zealously guarded, as they have a habit of disappearing. (They often reappear in the possession of a nearby musician, under circumstances suspiciously resembling theft.) Keeping the pencil sharp is another problem altogether — one of the few times that sharpness can be an asset. Courses in this art have recently been introduced at some of the more progressive music schools.

Performance The main reason for the getting together of any number of musicians, usually to perform a piece of music (ideally, all at the same time). It's the best excuse for a large, drunken party — although any excuse will do.

Piano 1. A cumbersome piece of furniture found in many homes, where playing it ensures the early departure of unwanted guests.
2. A dynamic level, quiet, many musicians find it almost impossible to achieve. And for them, the even quieter

dynamic level, pianissimo, is entirely a theoretical concept.

Piano tuner A person employed to come into the home, rearrange the furniture and annoy the cat. The tuner's chief purpose is to ascertain the breaking point of the piano strings.

Pitch

Pitch 1. The relative highness or lowness of a musical note, and the ability to control the same. For an interesting discussion of the curious overlap of terminology between music and baseball, the inquiring reader is referred to the seminal treatise on the subject: *Das kuriosen überlappisch Terminologichen zwishen Musik und Baseball und warum es Samstag immer regnet* (Munchen: Ashenbecker Verlag) 1897, rev. 1926. 2. Another name for tar — which, along with a bag of feathers, is an essential ingredient for punishing those performers (especially singers) unable to control the relative highness or lowness of a note.

Podium A raised platform given to conductors to make them feel more important than they really are. From the podium, the conductor can look over the orchestra and overlook its mistakes.

Polytonality A pathological disease most likely to affect composers of modern music. A mild form of atonality. Since one of its characteristics is the evidence of a sense of confusion, it's often hard to detect — that being the usual state of many musicians and composers. Nevertheless, this particular confusion tends to manifest itself in a desire to be "all things to all men," at least as regards key and key signature.

Prima donna The most important female role in an opera. This is, of course, largely a matter of opinion. By extension, the term has come to be applied to any singer who merely behaves as if hers is the most important role — that's to say, everyone. Derived from an Italian phrase that may be roughly translated as "pain in the neck," although some have a lower opinion. Not to be confused with pre-Madonna, that time period before the arrival of the pop star who elevated prima donna-ish behavior to an art form.

Principals In an opera company, orchestra or musical production, the term for the most important performers or singing roles. Not to be confused with principles, a set of moral guidelines often entirely lacking in such performers, and also in impresarios at contract time.

Prodigy A person who shows tremendous musical talent at a very early age. Mozart, one of music's greatest prodigies, set the example later followed by others by dying at age 36. Those wishing to be considered prodigy material would be well advised to die young, before it becomes apparent they aren't going to get any better, and while the reduced union rates for children still apply.

Program notes Short essays, filled with useless and

unverified (i.e. untrue) information about composers and their music, provided as a supplement to the performance. They are intended to furnish insight into the music, on the fanciful theory that a well-informed audience is an appreciative audience. In fact, it's probably better to keep audiences in the dark — figuratively speaking. They're already literally in the dark, which makes it impossible to read the program notes anyway. At any rate, all of this is a moot point, since the program will be changed at the last minute, and it will bear no relation to what's written in the notes.

Prodigy

Queen of the Night

Q.

Quartet 1. Formerly, all that remained of the Moscow Philharmonic Orchestra after its North American tour. Now, in these times of cutbacks, all that remains of just about any orchestra after the salary budget is set.
2. The number of players in most orchestras who are worth hanging on to anyway.

Quasi An Italian term for "almost," meaning "in the style of" (as in Beethoven's *Moonlight Sonata*, described as *quasi una fantasia* — as if it were a fantasia). Not to be confused with queasy, the sort of feeling a nervous performer might get before having to play Beethoven's *Moonlight Sonata*.

Quaver 1. The English term for the eighth note.
2. What nervous musicians do before a performance, especially one involving a lot of eighth notes.

Queen of the Night 1. A fearsome, domineering and imperious woman, Pamina's mother, in Mozart's *Magic Flute*.
2. Any fearsome, domineering and imperious soprano who sings the role.
3. Just about any singer you could name, usually female.

R

Racket 1. A Renaissance wind instrument with a very low range, resembling a coffee can with a double reed sticking out the top. Possibly so named because it makes a lot of noise.
2. In modern music, the best word to describe most of what you hear.

Radical bass 1. Same as fundamental bass — the bass line (often imaginary) derived from having each chord in its root position.
2. The type of singer who hung around Berkeley in the '60s.

Rank 1. In church organs, the term for a particular grouping of pipes.
2. Also in church organs, the term for the awful sound those pipes sometimes make.

Rant 1. An old English dance of the 17th century.
2. The kind of screaming fit or tantrum temperamental musicians are sometimes prone to, often after having to play (or worse, dance) too many of the above.

Rattle 1. A noisemaking toy given to amuse a fussy baby.
2. A small instrument used by percussion players — many of whom are just fussy babies anyway.

Recital A performance by a soloist or small group of musicians, more intimate and often shorter than a concert — but nevertheless still not short enough to avoid being tiresome. Often a farewell performance old musicians give before they die. Sometimes they die there, too. Not to be confused with rectal, a kind of intimate and intrusive medical examination often less painful to endure than some recitals.

Recitative Gossip set to music. A device in opera or oratorio for getting large chunks of narration over with quickly. Unfortunately, this leaves more time to be spent on long-winded arias. The musical equivalent of tile grouting or the wiring that strings together the lights on a Christmas tree. Recitatives (or "recits") are delivered in a style that combines singing with speaking and evokes the negative qualities of both. They are useful for conveying information (as distinct from arias, which convey only emotion or self-indulgence). *Recitativo accompagnato*, or *stromentato*, accompanies the singer with several orchestral instruments. Recits featuring the singer with only harpsicord and perhaps a bass instrument (cello, bassoon, double-B-flat contrakazoo or whatever) are called *recitativo secco*, from the Italian for "dry" (as opposed to the arias — which, with all that sobbing, are considerably more soggy).

Realism A concept theoretically desirable but practically never obtainable in opera. (See Verismo.)

Reeds A family of instruments that includes the clarinet, oboe, bassoon and kazoo. The name derives from the material that vibrates to produce the sound. Many reeds would be better off left in the swamp.

Refrain 1. That part of a song that keeps being repeated, *ad nauseam*.
2. What most performers should do.

Rehearsal Ideally, a meeting of musicians (and singers) for the purpose of becoming familiar with the music. In fact, a social occasion where little if any work is done. Most useful for the repetition of mistakes.

Rehearsal letter 1. A letter of the alphabet written into the score and the individual parts of a piece of music. The placement of the letter corresponds to the number of the bar, and is intended as a reference point to facilitate rehearsal. That's the theory, anyway. Unfortunately, the letter often appears at a different place in each part, leading to mass confusion.
2. A note from your mother explaining why you were late or missed last week's rehearsal.

Relative 1. The term used to describe a major and minor key that share the same key signature.
2. The person you might count on to attend your performance when no one else bothers to come — or at least to buy a ticket, if only out of a sense of family obligation.

Repertoire The large number of standard pieces of music with which an orchestral musician must claim to be familiar in order to secure a position in a major orchestra. Also, the pieces a singer is likely to forget at any given time. The American Civil War hero General Ulysses S. Grant made the definitive comment on repertoire when he remarked: "I only know two tunes. One of them is *Yankee Doodle*. The other one isn't."

Rescue opera 1. A genre of opera especially popular in 18th-century France with plotlines in which the hero and heroine escape from disastrous situations.
2. What someone should do to the whole art form before it goes completely down the tubes.

Resolution 1. In harmony, the successful movement from a discordant note to a more harmonious one.
2. In contract negotiations, pretty much the same situation (see Mediation).

Resonance A quality of tone that most musicians strive for, and that singers have in their head voice instead of brains (see Brain).

Rest 1. A short period of relative silence in an individual part, useful for turning pages, breathing, cleaning out spit valves, coughing and so forth. Rarely found in Baroque music, union regulations now exist to govern the number of rests required in each piece of music (usually one per bar, or 15 minutes of every hour).
2. What some of us need after being subjected to long performances.
3. The kind of home old musicians should be sent to when they're past their prime.

Rest

Rhapsody A heightened emotional state likely to interfere with a musician's practice time, not to mention sleep (see Lust, Passion).

Rheingold, Das An elaborate opera by Wagner, the first of four that make up the *Ring* cycle. Notable as the only opera in the standard repertoire to take place under water, which helps explain why it sounds so bloated, soggy and generally washed up.

Rhythm 1. A faculty in great demand and, unfortunately, in very short supply among those involved in music.
2. An unreliable method for curtailing the population of musicians.

Ring cycle The popular English name for the four

operas of Wagner's *Der Ring des Nibelungen*. Not to be confused with the rinse cycle, which is what you put your clothes through after sitting through an entire performance of Wagner's operas.

Ring des Nibelungen, Der A massive, four-opera cycle by Richard Wagner about a bunch of dwarfs, giants and spiteful Norse gods running around stealing each other's treasure and fighting over a magic decoder ring. (Imagine a bunch of kids arguing over the prize in a specially marked cereal box. Now imagine that at six times the volume and with a full orchestra. Got the idea?)

Rossini, Gioacchino One of the nicer of the big-name opera composers, an 18th-century Italian whose works include *The Barber of Seville*, *William Tell* and *The Thieving Magpie*. Enormously successful and popular (and just plain enormous, too), Rossini knew enough to quit while he was ahead — a bit of wisdom very few other composers have managed to acquire.

Round 1. A short, simple, repetitive piece of music similar to a canon, but less likely to misfire. 2. The shape eventually achieved by many musicians. (See Figure.)

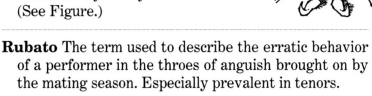

Rubato The term used to describe the erratic behavior of a performer in the throes of anguish brought on by the mating season. Especially prevalent in tenors.

Runs An ailment particularly prevalent among singers

of Baroque music, especially that of Bach and Handel. Can often be remedied by proper diet.

Runs

S

Sagbut 1. A brass instrument (also spelled sackbut), an early form of trombone. 2. A condition bound to afflict aging musicians unless they get regular exercise.

Sainete A form of comic opera popular in late 18th-century Spain, generally involving scenes with lowlife characters. Distinct from modern productions, where most of the lowlifes are either part of the production crew or in management.

Salieri, Antonio An Italian composer of operas and other genres working in 18th-century Vienna. Hugely popular in his own day but largely forgotten now except as the man who supposedly poisoned Mozart. Rimsky-Korsakov wrote a whole opera about him, based on a poem by Pushkin. And of course he's in that great movie *Amadeus*, played by F. Murray Abraham. Salieri didn't actually poison Mozart (the fact Mozart had health problems and later bought the farm is pretty much his own fault) but that hardly makes the story less entertaining. It just goes to show, you should take your fame wherever you can get it.

Salome A Biblical "bad girl" and the title character of Richard Strauss's operatic adaptation of the famous Oscar Wilde play. Does the *Dance of the Seven Veils* and gets the head of John the Baptist served up on a platter (so not the kind of girl you'd want to take home to Mother). Not to be confused with salami — which, although likewise often served up on a platter, is generally considered more appropriate dinnertime fare.

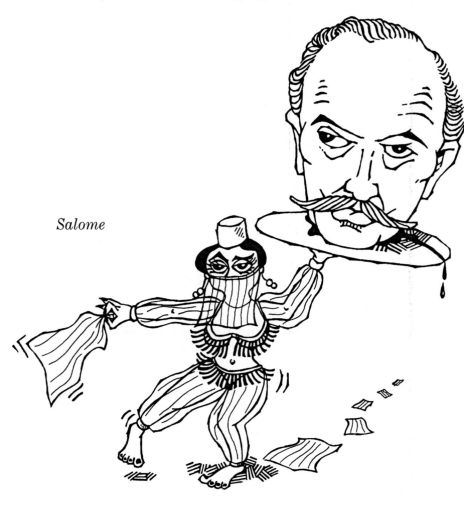

Salome

Sanglot A fancy French term for "sob," the kind of cheap, theatrical device opera singers often resort to, especially if they can't remember the words.

Scale 1. A stepwise collection of notes often played as a warmup exercise.
2. The rate of pay determined by the union and given to musicians who diligently practise their warmup exercises.

Scat 1. A style of singing found especially in jazz, characterized by rapid nonsense syllables.
2. A command for getting rid of unwanted animals, and sometimes singers repeating rapid nonsense syllables.

Scene 1. The setting or location of the action in a passage of opera. Composers try to include them to make the drama flow more smoothly.
2. A period of great discomfort and enormous tactical advantage created by a singer dissatisfied with the current rate of pay, size of dressing room, billing on the marquee or whatever. Managers try to avoid them to make the production flow more smoothly.

Schweigsame Frau, Die A comic opera (*The Silent Woman*) by Richard Strauss, first performed in Dresden in 1935. In my opinion, the world of opera would benefit greatly from having a whole lot more silent women (and men, too).

Score 1. An amalgamation of all the individual parts, transposed into the key of C, so no one else can understand it. This is what conductors conduct from, and they are supposed to have studied it carefully. Most conductors, however, don't know the score.
2. What some of the musicians hope to do with some of the other musicians when the performance is over.

Scoring 1. The art of assigning parts to various instruments or singers.
2. The finer art of assigning one's private parts to various instrumentalists or singers (see Action, Double action).

Serial music Not to be confused with early-morning, or cereal music. The result of a method of composition using all 12 notes of the scale in some established order. Despite this, the result is often chaos.

Serse The hero and title character of Handel's only comic opera. He gets to sing his big love song (*Ombra mai fù*) to a tree — which isn't actually as funny as it sounds, but it is pretty amusing. (For more fascinating information on this topic, see Largo, Handel's)

Serva padrona, La A little intermezzo written by Pergolesi in 1733 that's considered absolutely crucial to the development of *opera buffa* in the 18th century. Everybody says so, so it must be true. Pay attention, this might be on the exam.

Shake 1. In early music, another name for trill.
2. In all music, an attack of nerves a performer succumbs to before going on stage (and sometimes while on stage).

Sharp 1. Adjective used to describe a tone that's slightly above pitch (see Flat. Not so easily misconstrued.)
2. An adjective used to describe a nattily attired colleague.
3. What managers and agents have to be to stay ahead of the game.

Sharps Little marks that look like this: # and that would be useful for playing Xs and Os during the more boring moments of a performance if they weren't so small. They're similar to flats, but different. Their function is to raise a note by a semitone (more or less). They may also be gathered to form key signatures. For an explanation of the double-sharp, read the entry for Flats and figure it out for yourself. There may be a short quiz at the end of this book.

Siegfried The hero and title character of the third opera in Wagner's *Ring* cycle. Siegfried is the illegitimate son of an incestuous liaison between a twin brother and sister, Siegmund and Sieglinde, who got it on together in the previous opera, *Die Walküre*. (This is the kind of thing that drives the "family values" types to hysterics — admittedly a short trip.)

Singer A special type of musician, notable for the inability to count at all. Unlike other musicians, who must rely on an instrument to produce sound, singers use only what they call "the vocal apparatus" (and what ordinary people would call "the voice"). There are certain inherent advantages and disadvantages: On the one hand, singers wishing to improve their technique can't simply buy better instruments — but then some of the carrying cases are so much more attractive.

Sleepwalking 1. An operatic plot device (most notably in Bellini's *La sonnambula*) and a useful ruse for leaving a bad performance early, if you can get away with it.

Snob, musical Someone who pretends to know more about music than we pretend to.

Solo A device that makes it easier to place the blame for mistakes entirely on one individual. The other device that facilitates this is called the conductor.

Soloists Individuals whose egos are larger than both their brains and their ability combined, and equalled in some cases only by their greed. Soloists can be of two types, either (a) good or (b) bad. The latter are more common. In fact, the former exist only in theoretical treatises, and have never been known to exist in real life. Certainly never in real performances.

Sonata form The development of sonata form (also called sonata allegro form or first-movement form) is one of the most fascinating topics in the study of music, since it combines elements of history, theory, analysis and composition. It also involves all of the major composers of Western music. I wish we had more time to talk about it.

Soprano The highest vocal line, sung by women (but see Treble). Sopranos have a tendency to sing sharp and to sound like fingernails scraped on chalkboard. Not to be confused with soaprano, a woman who sprayed her throat from the wrong bottle on the bathroom counter. Derived from the Latin *superius*, which means "highest." This has given many sopranos a superiority complex, exceedingly unfounded. Sopranos tend to be the most feeble-minded of all the singing voices. This may be explained by the fact that notes of higher frequency travel directly to the brain (but see Brain) and cause rapid decay. In opera and other works, sopranos are usually the heroines, or sometimes the heroine's best friend, faithful servant, long-lost sister or whatever. Generally pretty clueless, the operatic soprano's main job is to stand around looking good while others fight over her. Sometimes gets to die in the end — tragically and at great length.

Soaprano

Sotto voce An Italian term (literally "under the voice") directing performers to sing very quietly. With most singers, this means turning down the volume so it doesn't actually peel paint off the walls, just loosens it a bit.

Sound 1. A polite term for noise.

2. A type of mental attitude rarely obtained by musicians, even more rarely by conductors and never by singers.

Species 1. In early music, a term for designating various classes of counterpoint.

2. A term for designating various classes of musicians. (Usually the human species — but with some of them, you can't always tell.)

Stop 1. A device on the organ, which changes the sound of a note from disagreeable to annoying.

2. What organists should do to improve their playing (see Refrain).

Stringendo Also string-endo. The term applied to a deceased violin.

Strings 1. A family of instruments that includes the violin, viola, cello, double-bass and yo-yo. The strings used in producing the sound were originally manufactured out of catgut. This may be responsible for their ear-piercing tone, which continues even in these days of synthetic string material. Ancient violin makers believed the best strings were made from female cats in heat, as evidenced by the violin's characteristic screech.

2. What many musicians need to pull in order to land a decent job — or even any job.

T

Takt The German term for "beat" or "measure," meaning the underlying pulse of a piece of music. Not to be confused with tact, meaning an essential quality of diplomacy and consideration that most musicians lack.

Tantrum An emotional display of temper, impatience and selfishness, invoked when reason fails to attain the desired goal. A favorite device of children and soloists (a needless distinction) who want to get their own way. Like children, soloists often find that if a tantrum doesn't work, two tantrums usually do.

Te Deum A particular work set by various composers for use during a church service. Not to be confused with tedium, the feeling you often get from listening to such works.

Temperament 1. A set of guidelines for tuning instruments, chiefly keyboards.
2. The state of mind that quickly deteriorates when such guidelines are applied incompetently.

Tempo The speed at which music travels. Said to be controlled by the conductor, but in reality by the players. It may vary from piece to piece, and certainly from player to player. It's always faster in performance than it has been in rehearsal, usually by a factor of two.

Tenor A high-pitched male voice, akin to screaming. A man with a high voice and an even higher opinion of himself. Extremely rare, so usually sung by frustrated baritones whose reach exceeds their grasp. Tenors have a tendency to sing off-pitch, out of time and out of control and to sound like a strangulating cat. Derived from the Latin *tenor*, which means "to hold" (compare tenacious, tenuous, tentative). In comic opera, the tenor usually gets to play the hero, adored by the people and lucky in the romance department. This can lead to problems off stage, where tenors mistakenly assume the same privileges still apply. In tragic opera, the tenor still gets to play the hero but rarely gets the girl, because either one or other of them dies, sometimes both. (Strangely, they never seem to feel this privilege should apply off stage as well. Too bad.)

Tie 1. A small, curved mark that joins together two notes.
2. A small black piece of cloth that joins together the front of a musician's shirt collar.
3. In duets, the only diplomatic way to decide the winner.

Time 1. An important aspect of musical notation. (See Tempo.)
2. One of the four dimensions of the universe, which physicists theorize moves forward at a constant pace. Audience members and musicians, especially those stuck listening to (or worse, performing in) bad performances, know this not to be true. There, time may drag to a near standstill (or pass quite quickly once you've fallen asleep). Obviously, the full effect of music, especially bad music, on Einstein's *General Theory of Relativity* has yet to be studied.

Tone 1. That aspect of a singer's performance you can compliment when you can't understand the words (see Diction).
2. The interval of the distance between two adjacent notes. Can be either a whole tone or a semitone. Occasional use of quarter-tones has not been successful, since musicians have difficulty dealing with frac-

tions smaller than halves.

Tone cluster A kind of chordal orgy, a smorgasbord of musical notes. First discovered by a very well-endowed lady pianist, while leaning forward to turn a page.

Tonic A medicinal libation usefully consumed before a performance — and even more usefully so afterward.

Touch 1. In keyboard and other instruments, a part of the action that contributes to tone quality.
2. In rehearsal or performance, the kind of action that can get you in trouble if unwelcome or misinterpreted.

Transposition 1. The act of moving the relative pitch of a piece of music that's too low for the basses up to a point where it's too high for the sopranos.
2. A method of ensuring that no musician will be able to read a part belonging to another musician, by writing each part in a different key. Through some miracle not as yet understood by theorists, the parts usually sound right together. The conductor retaliates by transposing everything into the key of C (see Score) to confuse the musicians, and because that's the only key that most conductors can read, even a little bit. The main purpose of transposition is to provide work for copyists.

Travesti The Italian term for the so-called "pants role" in opera in which a female singer plays a male character (this rarely happens the other way around), such as Romeo in Bellini's *I Capuletti*, Smeton in Donizetti's *Anna Bolena*, Cherubino in Mozart's *Marriage of Figaro* and so on. Not to be confused with travesty, a term that refers to all operas in general.

Treble A small boy used especially in Anglican church choirs to sing the highest vocal line (under other circumstances sung by a soprano). Those who favor this type of choral sound maintain that all the effort it takes to properly train small boys is worthwhile, because the end result is so pleasing — and because they are usually the boys' mothers. In addition to the usual skills of sight reading and interpretation, boys must be taught forms of self-discipline such as bladder control. Often, the former is easer than the latter. Not to be confused with trouble, although the two generally amount to the same thing.

Triangle 1. A small high-pitched instrument used by percussionists chiefly to annoy the rest of the orchestra.
2. A romantic configuration not advised for musicians wishing to avoid heartache, embarrassment, financial ruin or legal proceedings (see Double action).

Trill The musical equivalent of an epileptic seizure. A minor earthquake in the region of a particular note, said to be ornamental, but often merely a substitute for accuracy. Singers are especially fond of trilling, since it saves them the bother of having to learn the tunes properly.

Trio sonata An instrumental piece popular in the Baroque, so called because it has parts for four players. This is the same sort of logic that accounts for the theorist's calling the combined intervals of an octave and a third a 10th (8+3=10 — what could be more sensible than that?). The inherent fallibility of this reasoning has not seemed to dismay musicians over the centuries, so we shouldn't let it trouble us now. Strangely enough, musicians' inability to count properly disappears whenever they're calculating their wages.

Trombone A slide whistle with delusions of grandeur.

Tuning 1. A means by which orchestras establish harmonic consensus — largely as a result of compromise, sometimes bribery or coercion.
2. An abstract concept with which singers have very little firsthand knowledge.

Tuxedo A type of ill-fitting black suit worn by male musicians during a performance. It's purchased at a local Salvation Army store (or — preferably — borrowed from another musician) and must be at least 10 years old. It's either too large or too small, too baggy or too tight. Footwear accompanying the tuxedo is very occasionally a pair of black dress shoes (rarely polished), but more often sneakers, brown loafers or sandals. The addition of a questionable white shirt and a bowtie (either black or rainbow-colored) completes the outfit. The ownership of a tuxedo is mandatory for male musicians — much like a fez for Shriners. The female equivalent of the tuxedo is any dress, usually (but not always) knee-length or longer, that's vaguely black (i.e. black, grey, brown, blue, purple, chartreuse, etc.).

U

Unessential notes A relative term — one that never applies to your own notes, but only to those of other performers (see Wrong notes).

Unison The sound of two or more musicians performing the same note or part at exactly the same time. (Note: Like the speed of light, absolute zero and various other philosophical and scientific Holy Grails, this is a theoretical concept only. It's never actually been achieved in a real performance.)

Upbeat 1. A conductor's motion that prepares for a rhythmic accent.
2. What conductors must remain to encourage their performers, even when things are falling apart (often the result of conductors forgetting to make the right motions to prepare for rhythmic accents).

Upright 1. A style of piano, smaller than a grand, found in homes and rehearsal halls.
2. What performers and audiences should remain for the duration of the performance (except for those in a dying scene).

Vibrato

V

Valhalla 1. In Norse mythology, the abode of the gods up in the sky and the final reward for heroic warriors. A place of wine, women, song, feasting and merriment — pretty much like the Legion hall on a rowdy Saturday night, but with mead and swordplay instead of beer and poker.

2. In Wagner's *Ring* cycle, the elaborate palace built in the first opera (*Das Rheingold*) for Wotan and Fricka

by the giants Fasolt and Fafner. Like most contractors, they end up haggling over the final price, and they aren't around in the end when the whole thing falls apart from bad workmanship.

Valkyrie 1. In Norse mythology, one of a troop of fierce warrior women on flying horses, an early and impressive example of affirmative action in the military — a kind of militant cleaning lady on steroids. Ferocious but tidy, the Valkyries protect warriors in battle and, when they goof up, carry away the dead to Valhalla, keeping the battlefield from getting too cluttered. In *Die Walküre* and the rest of Wagner's *Ring* cycle, the Valkyries are led by Brünnhilde, a moody but endearingly loyal pyromaniac with a strong Joan of Arc complex.

Valve A means of changing the direction of the flow of air (and spit) in the tube of a brass instrument. Similar to a highway detour, but less likely to require a map.

Variations 1. The sorts of tunes written by composers who can never make up their minds.
2. Accidental alterations to a tune by which performers display their arrogance and disrespect for composers. In practice, every piece is a variation, since musicians consider performing it the same way each time would be a sign of weakness.

Verismo A style of writing opera that attempts to make the characters and situations more lifelike and realistic. Since the terms "opera" and "realism" are mutually exclusive, *verismo* — like Santa Claus and the Tooth Fairy — can never really exist at all.

Vibraphone A xylophone with stage fright.

Vibrato A technique used by certain instruments, said to add warmth and body to the tone, and used by singers to hide the fact that they're on the wrong pitch. The musical equivalent of those wobbly restaurant tables with one leg just slightly shorter than the others — and just about as annoying, too.

Viol One of a family of bowed string instruments, popular in the Renaissance, that became the forerunners of the modern violin family. Opinion is divided on which of the two instruments, ancient or modern, is more vile than the other.

Viola A relative of the violin, a sort of poor cousin.

Votre toast

Violin The squeakiest member of the string family. It tends to get its way in an orchestra because violins outnumber the other instruments.

Virginal A keyboard instrument similar to the harpsichord, so called because of the sorts of ladies who were supposed to have played it in the 16th century — and if you believe that, you'll believe anything.

Voice A singer's chief instrument of commanding respect, whether on stage singing or off stage demanding a larger dressing room.

Voluntary The name given to a piece for organ often played at the end of a church service. The terminology is puzzling and ironic, since under such circumstances one's decision to endure the assault is far from voluntary.

Votre toast 1. The name of Escamillo's famous *Toreador Song* in Act II of Bizet's *Carmen*.
2. Having spent the night with a cute French singer, what you might offer in the morning for breakfast.

W

Wagner 1. A student character in various operatic versions of the Faust legend. (See Hell.) **2.** A German composer, Richard Wagner, of long, overblown operas. (See Hell.)

Walküre, Die See Brünnhilde, Valkyrie.

Wind The essential ingredient needed to produce sound from many instruments. It's possessed in large quantities by conductors, who have very little need for it, except for bellowing at the players.

Wind machine A large, barrel-shaped device for imitating the sound of rushing wind. Used by composers such as Richard Strauss in his tone-poem *Don Quixote* and, of course, in the person of all opera singers.

Wooden In opera, an adjective to describe the construction material of some of the instruments and the acting style of most of the singers.

Woodwinds A family of instruments so called because its members are made of wood. This includes the flute (made of silver), the saxophone (made of brass) and the bassoon (often made of plastic). The woodwind family includes all the members of the reed family, as well as others, such as the flute, that would otherwise feel left out. Like most families, the members often quarrel.

Words Essential elements for conveying mood, narrative and emotion. Carefully chosen by librettists and composers and wantonly disregarded by singers.

Wotan The chief god in Norse mythology and a central character in Wagner's *Ring* cycle. A demanding but inspiring leader but at heart a doting father, some musicologists see Wotan as representing the absent father figure Wagner longed for in his own life. Far too Freudian and weird to think about — a topic best avoided altogether.

Wrong notes A relative term (see Unessential notes), applying only to those examples performed by someone else. Wrong notes you perform yourself are always referred to as "ornaments."

Woodwind

X

Xenophobia The irrational mistrust and dislike of foreigners — a condition that might result from watching too many operas or other musical performances.

Xerxes The hero of one of Handel's operas and a man with a seriously weird tree obsession. It's a *castrato* role, which may or may not have anything to do with it — depending how much faith you put in Freud. (See Serse.)

Xylophone An instrument of the percussion family that in both appearance and sound resembles a pile of old kindling. Its chief claim to fame is that its name begins with an "x" — the only instrument so honored (well, except for the xylomarimba, but that's pretty much the same thing). Consequently, it's extremely useful for compilers of music dictionaries.

Y

Yawn The act of opening the mouth wide to take in breath. Usually the result of boredom or lack of sleep, it's generally considered bad form to yawn during a concert — especially if you're one of the performers.

Yodelling A bizarre form of vocal warbling found in certain regions of the Swiss Alps during traditional ceremonies and on opera stages all the time.

Z

Z The sound of contentment made by musicians after a taxing performance, and by audiences during (especially opera and those really weird modern composers). Usually found in the plural, thus: Zzzzzz. Often accompanied by a snore.

Zaide An unfinished opera by Mozart — which, had he completed it, would have been more interesting to scholars and more useful for the purposes of this dictionary.

Zarzuela A fancy Spanish term for short operettas, usually comic but sometimes tragic, and a useful word for impressing your friends at your next cocktail party.

Zauberflöte, Die See *Magic Flute, The.*

Zauberoper A German term ("magic opera") for operas with supernatural or unbelievable elements: fire-breathing dragons, magic spells, honest politicians — whatever.

Zitti, zitti 1. A trio sung by Almaviva, Figaro and Rosina in Act II of Rossini's *The Barber of Seville.*
2. A facial outbreak that's going to put a damper on your hopes for a big date.

Zukunftsmusik A highfalutin German word meaning "music of the future," the term often used by Wagner and his followers to describe his music. A depressing concept, really. If Wagner's operas represent the music of the future, what's the point in going on?

Zauberoper

BOOKS BY DAVID W. BARBER
WITH ILLUSTRATIONS
BY DAVE DONALD

Bach, Beethoven and the Boys:
Music History as It Ought to Be Taught
(1986, republished 2009 by Indent Publishing,
also available as an Indent ebook, 2011)

When the Fat Lady Sings:
Opera History as It Ought to Be Taught
(1990, also available as an Indent Publishing ebook, 2012)

If It Ain't Baroque:
More Music History as It Ought to Be Taught
(1992, also available as an Indent Publishing ebook, 2012)

Getting a Handel on Messiah
(1995, also available as an Indent Publishing ebook, 2011)

Tenors, Tantrums and Trills:
An Opera Dictionary
(1996)

Tutus, Tights and Tiptoes:
Ballet History as It Ought to Be Taught
(2000, also available as an Indent Publishing ebook, 2012)

Accidentals on Purpose:
A Musician's Dictionary
(Indent Publishing 2011,
also available as an Indent ebook, 2012)

BOOKS BY DAVID W. BARBER

Better Than it Sounds:
A Dictionary of Humorous Musical Quotations
(1998)

The Last Laugh:
Essays and Oddities in the News
(2000, also available as an
Indent Publishing ebook, 2011)

Quotable Alice
(2001, also available as an Indent Publishing ebook, 2011)

Quotable Sherlock
(2001, also available as an Indent Publishing ebook, 2011)

Quotable Twain
(2002, also available as an Indent Publishing ebook, 2012)

The Music Lover's Quotation Book
(2003)

The Adventure of the Sunken Parsley:
and other stories of Sherlock Holmes
(Indent Publishing ebook, 2011)

Better Than it Sounds:
The Music Lover's Quotation Book
(Indent Publishing ebook, 2012)

ABOUT THE AUTHOR

DAVID W. BARBER is a journalist and musician and the author of more than a dozen books of music (including *Accidentals on Purpose: A Musician's Dictionary*, *Bach, Beethoven and the Boys*, *When the Fat Lady Sings* and *Getting a Handel on Messiah*) and literature (including *Quotable Sherlock* and *Quotable Twain*). Formerly entertainment editor of the *Kingston Whig-Standard* and editor of *Broadcast Week* magazine at the Toronto *Globe and Mail*, he's now a copy editor at the *National Post* and a freelance writer, editor and composer. As a composer, his works include two symphonies, a jazz Mass based on the music of Dave Brubeck, a Requiem, several short choral and chamber works and various vocal-jazz songs and arrangements. He sings with the Toronto Chamber Choir and Cantores Fabularum and a variety of other choirs on occasion. In a varied career, among his more interesting jobs have been short stints as a roadie for Pope John Paul II, a publicist for Prince Rainier of Monaco and a backup singer for Avril Lavigne.

Find him on the Web at bachbeethoven.com
or indentpublishing.com

ABOUT THE CARTOONIST

DAVE DONALD can't remember when he didn't scrawl his little marks on most surfaces, so it doesn't come as much of a surprise that he now makes a living doing just that. He is currently balancing a freelance career in publication design with his more abstruse artistic pursuits. This book represents his first of seven illustrative collaborations with David Barber.